WHAT TO WEAR WHEN SURVIVING A LION ATTACK

WHAT TO WEAR WHEN SURVIVING A LION ATTACK

Paola Ferrante

Mansfield Press

Printed in Canada

Library and Archives Canada Cataloguing in Publication

Title: What to wear when surviving a lion attack / Paola Ferrante.
Names: Ferrante, Paola, author.
Description: Poems.
Identifiers: Canadiana 20190102578 | ISBN 9781771262248 (softcover)
Classification: LCC PS8611.E755 W53 2019 | DDC C811/.6—dc23

Cover Image: Wounded Lion, Raden Saleh, 1839
Author Photo: Pat Bolduc
Design: Denis De Klerck

The publication of *What To Wear When Surviving A Lion Attack* has been generously supported by the Canada Council for the Arts and the Ontario Arts Council.

ONTARIO ARTS COUNCIL
CONSEIL DES ARTS DE L'ONTARIO
an Ontario government agency
un organisme du gouvernement de l'Ontario

Canada Council for the Arts
Conseil des arts du Canada

Mansfield Press Inc.
25 Mansfield Avenue, Toronto, Ontario, Canada M6J 2A9
Publisher: Denis De Klerck
www.mansfieldpress.net

For my mother

TABLE OF CONTENTS

9 THINGS SHE WANTS
11 WEDDING DAY, CIRÇA MY MOTHER
13 D.C. AL CODA (FROM THE HEAD TO THE TAIL)
14 LET'S TALK
15 FIRST GIRL/FINAL GIRL
16 PRIME TIME HORROR STORY
17 THE MANIPULATOR
19 GOING SOUTH
20 RATIONING
22 HOMING
23 THE MERE EXPOSURE EFFECT, OR HOW TO MAKE MEN LIKE YOU
24 TO MY PEEPING TOM
26 MISSED HER RIGHT
28 SOUND BITES
30 THREE MONKEYS
32 BEAUTY AND THE BEAST
33 IMPOSSIBLE SPLIT, OR WHAT TO WEAR WHEN SURVIVING A LION ATTACK
34 PENDULUM
36 EVEN THIS POEM IS BLUE
37 THE STARTER
38 NIGHTS OF THE LIVING POSSUM
40 THE TRUE CONFESSIONS OF BUFFALO BILL
42 SPECIMEN
43 ON MY MOTHER'S TERMS
45 WHEN READING HAMLET IN MY THIRTIES I ANSWERED FOR GERTRUDE
47 OF WEATHERING VIEWED THROUGH THE EYELETS OF A SPOON BUSK

49 THE ACCIDENT
51 MIRROR MIRROR MOTHER MOTHER
53 AS TOLD DURING A ROUTINE POLICE INVESTIGATION
54 DELUSIONAL DOMINATING PERSONALITY DISORDER
55 SISTER/HOOD
56 THE POLITICS OF LEFTOVERS
57 ON THE PROCESS OF MAKING OMELETTES
58 GESTATIONAL STAGE
60 THE EMERGENCY MANOEUVRES OF BLUEBEARD 6
61 DOPPELGANGER
63 YO YO FOR BEGINNERS
65 DIFFERENTIAL DIAGNOSIS
66 ON NOT HAVING A BABY
68 CHOOSE YOUR OWN ADVENTURE
69 IF THE LEFT KNEE ITCHES
70 BY OMISSION
72 WITCH HUNT
73 GENERALIZED DISORDER
75 ON EXITING THE LOOP
77 BRIARS
78 ME TOO
79 LAWS OF MOTION
81 EXTINCTION

84 ACKNOWLEDGEMENTS

THINGS SHE WANTS

Unconditioned stimulus is touch. Unconditioned stimulus provokes a response, the expulsion of fluid from the Skene glands through and around the human female urethra as in when kissing as in when fucking as in when his fingers touch the most sensitive scalp while pulling her hair. Conditioned stimulus is then paired with unconditioned stimulus. If a dog, a female dog, is accustomed to being fed and salivates for food when the man plays a tone, consistently, suddenly her mouth is not her own. The conditioned stimulus is paired with the unconditioned stimulus like with the dog and the tone, as in fucking is paired with loving or blue and yellow roses or his grandmother's ring, as in fucking is paired with bedroom sets from Ikea, matching towels are paired with Thanksgiving dinner which is paired with the first baby named Aidan, boy or girl, it doesn't matter; these things she is supposed to want. The conditioned stimulus then provokes a response all by itself. Take a bridge. If a woman, a human woman, is scared of heights, her heart rate up, her breathing rate up and she meets a man on a bridge, she interprets the sensation. If a woman is scared and meets a man on a bridge she might think she is aroused. Stimuli do not interpret themselves. But if a dog is scared and meets a man, she barks. If a dog, a female dog, is scared she will run away and the man will try to control her fear; he uses treats, he uses dinners, he uses cuddles, he uses kisses. But if a bitch is scared and she bites he uses hurt, the way you bruise a fruit, slowly, on the inside, so no one notices until the pith is peeled back. Then the conditioned stimulus elicits the response that was previously only given by the unconditioned stimulus. As in when she sees their new duvet, their home, she gets wet, she cries. As in then somehow fucking is paired with fighting is paired with hitting is paired with the thing to hit with like the riding crop. A jockey cannot hit a horse, a female horse, anywhere except on the rump or the flank with a riding crop but when it comes to the woman, the human woman, he breaks the rules and no one will believe her. But if a horse meets a man on the bridge, she could crush him. If a woman meets a man and she is aroused and then scared the conditioned stimulus changes. As in fucking is paired with bruising is paired with touching is paired with choking and loving and bruising and touching and choking elicit a hemorrhage of fluids: semen, urine, blood. The fluids are like words when her mouth is not her own; these things she does not choose to want. If she is scared she is supposed to want to run but she runs and comes back and then runs and comes back and comes back and comes back. It takes twelve times to leave. Twelve times because it is worth it to remember that the unconditioned stimulus is paired with the boy or girl named Aidan, with Christmas lights together, with the thing they call future. It is worth it to remember that the man is paired with loving is paired with hitting is paired with bruising is paired with waking up in the dark to the sounds of warm breathing instead of quiet, instead of walking the suspension bridge alone.

WEDDING DAY, CIRCA MY MOTHER

When she was in white she was a bride, like a bird beloved.
When a bird is in white she learns she is his
dove. A dove who is mother
can make her own milk, also white in theory
though none of what milk is made of reflects
any more than any other part; she knows she makes it
through temporary starvation. She knows in theory
white light is all light like rainbows, a trick
of the rain; she knows

rarely can white light reflect on
nimbostratus clouds. There, air is smooth
but ground visibility minimal. There is no rain above rain clouds
because of gravity; the situation
is she should have been dry in theory

she should have wanted the weight
of gravity, a thickening of belly, picture
it in black and white ultrasound. In a white dress her pictures in black
and white, not sepia, where black is an absence of light

upstairs in the attic, where black
ink to page could have been.
In black she wanted
to know why
should she lie
like Lilith with his weight

when all
he wanted
for her was to grow
down

why
black, an absence
of light, is all
colours mixed

together, forever. But in white she was beloved, whether white
was wedding dress or sheet or shroud she was the other
half, who would not slash,
half Amazon, half
human.
She was human, with man, with human,
a capacity for having
relations.

And when she asked why
he never saw the
refraction of light

from all colours
mixed together, how black
is additive. His answer

was in black and white.
A wife is not a bird; she does not fly

upstairs. She settles
down, becomes
a black hole,
collapsing in
on herself.

D.C. AL CODA (FROM THE HEAD TO THE TAIL)

She was told one note followed another,
white-lipped gloves for communion's
waltz, her parts always backwards
and in heels.

She thought she wanted to sing.

Then it was blues from a cliff
in Katmandu in her summer of Joplin,
searching for one good man.
Like the nightingale

she met an emperor. He heard
only sex lips, some siren, wanted her
wings pinned like that nude of Monroe.
Then she sang like a bird's syrinx,

two notes at once.

When he took her
apart he said it's only natural.
She wanted to know why
he said she wanted,
she never wanted,
a catch in the throat he said
you be quiet;

even with those lips
only male songbirds sing.

Then my mother had to sing.
She sang the way of mechanical
birds. If you wind her up,
but only if you wind her.

LET'S TALK

Forget about the Dead Sea;
Florida's a hot spot for *naegleria fowleri*,
an amoeba that eats brains. You can't see it

but I'm losing density. I know what arms
should feel like, first-time campfire,
Georgian Bay, my bright beach summers

how yellow warms through feet. Remember
words but not the tingling, removal of skin
like paper cuts you tell me everything is fine.

This is the problem with living in a snow globe,
seismic levels of serotonin adjust at random,
threat of meltdown, then blast—a change of scene

you say, will do me good. Florida's nice
this time of year. But I'm not ready
for things to be beautiful, fallout
coating palm trees, sunsets.

Try to seek shade now, I wear
sunglasses at all times, exposed to ultra violent,
like warnings on old microwaves;
say you love me,
but don't stand too close.

FIRST GIRL/FINAL GIRL

On Friday the 13th I could have been Sandra Dier,
lips gashed up
in six shades of red
technicolor, waiting
for the knife, close-up

on a name no one
will recognize. Just like no one really knows
the identity of the bikinied teen,
saline breasts ready to burst,
going from side to side before
going under. On Halloween
I could have been Kelly Meeker,
a pin-up peeled back
á la Buffalo Bill, stripped

to keep me
from telling how being gorgeous

doesn't keep me
warm-blooded. When Jaws attacks
he doesn't leave much
to work with.

Of course, with all required surgeries
there are side effects: bruising, numbness,
a sense you should stay
out of the water.

When he attacked he didn't wear a mask,
forehead muscles
paralysed when I was told to scream;
I want to say it
could have been
the whole thing happened
to somebody else.

PRIME TIME HORROR STORY

When they report abandoned car seats used
to lure female motorists to locations next to
a wooded field or grassy opening
I know the way the story's going like
little girls repeat to make Bloody Mary
come out in the bathroom mirror.
Every time she looks she sees
scratches from what the man
in the window pulls out of his pocket,
not sure if he wants her blood on the car.
It's the man upstairs where they say
a woman's place is, calling to say
have you checked the children
why haven't you aren't you glad
you didn't turn on the t.v.?

See what's happening in America.
There's a hook-handed man
ready to tear her with coat hangers
down an alley, says he's concerned
with the state
of the children.
She's heard it before,
from the babysitter,
around a campfire.
Little girls are always told
the killer is right

inside the house.

THE MANIPULATOR

With Freud the problem lay
in talking, despite sewing
machines or equitation, like Anna O.
I could not
conjugate.

You thoughtfully provided
directions on posture
most conducive
to achieving

muscular contractions induced
without sensation on skin.
This vibrating cure at first
was one intended

for male
nerve centres, primarily
the spine. You told me

lean forward, like riding
a bike at 3000 vibrations a minute
which the larynx with airstream passing
between two folds

coming together
can neither match
nor exceed.

But you would hear of nothing
else.

Anna called it chimney sweeping,
this private theatre, while Freud believed
her present

actions just infinitives, split
when speaking of herself

unable to use
a subject, completely
mute then piecing
words together

edgewise. But you said forget
about a talking cure.
Upsuck theory dictates
I'd take in
what you're giving

through negative pressure
under your hand all it got me
was you thinking I'm Cleopatra
in some seventies porn,

a magic wand for pelvic massage really
a gourd of angry bees
inserted inside herself,
forgetting

her voice
was that of a diplomat.
Hysterical paroxysm called
by any other name

would smell, you said,
a bit fishy,

like the origin of hysteria
or the daughter's disease
to please. An inability to say

when it comes to Freud the problem
with Anna O.
was he just wanted
to keep talking.

GOING SOUTH

In case of armageddon, learn your knots. There is the rolling hitch, the sheet bend, a running bowline called the king. A running bowline can be used to climb a wall, tie down a boat, hang the swing for future children; a running bowline can be used to make a noose. Learn to tie the knot, but don't bother with untying; that's not what you learned in church. I am told the clock is ticking. In the desert at noon there's no need for a fire; you can fry an egg on a rock. In the desert, I learned to milk a cactus, seek shade from packing crates, string Christmas lights on bunkers. I learned to start a fire with cartons of eggs, start a fire when there is no longer a need. Things will be better next time. Eventually light comes through heat, illusion of wet convection from hot asphalt, or the exhaustion of a jet. I'm told we looked so happy once. Capture it on camera, like so many sunshines, frozen.

That time we went fishing, you tied a bumper knot to catch the bait; the bait was eggs, like breakfast. Like breakfast there were always eggs, always sunny side up, for us. I'm told we looked so happy once. Falling overboard, you said to keep my mouth shut, above the water. The last time I made eggs there was a tiny chicken, red, with almost feet; I cracked the yolk. Things will be better next time. There are ways to keep from drowning, empty out the diaphragm, drink, forget a deeper breath. Remember a mirage is not the water; a mirage means to admire. A mirage means learn prevailing winds, check the water's surface, see on what side debris has settled. Divination is preservation, not what you learned in Scouts; lines drawn on an analog clock directly between hour hand and twelve are metaphor more than cardinal direction. When I don't like where this is going find true north without a compass; use duct tape, a cork from that last bottle of champagne. Pucker up, wait for it to rain. I am told remember congratulations. Even when we're headed in opposite directions, remember eggs, sunny side up. Now any unconscious move is the difference between going south or otherwise, between loosening the knot or otherwise. This is the difference between thirst and drowning, even in a body of water that isn't.

RATIONING

I have never killed anyone except
a rabbit
my mother

called Evie. Tiny
pink like the rest
she adopted.

When the rabbit stopped
feeding in our backyard, when a predator
found the burrow

it's not like she wanted to do it.
When you're older you'll understand

it's less cruel; only a cuckoo bird
does not want her egg, will trick
it into another's nest.

I wonder now if mother enjoyed it,
her hands that made all
movement stop
after she came outside,

the way she taught me
once to hold
a pen, said she could have

become what
she'll never know.
Once I came

she lost
sleep, gained interrupted
dreams. Still, she said,

that's love, a natural choice
between caloric needs
of a burying beetle

and her young,
regurgitated, feeding the mother between
the mother and the offspring,

umbilical ties that bind so
you are no longer
alone. When you have your own,

you'll understand
we all make choices.

HOMING

A man adapts a pigeon for getting without knowing. A man who is a scientist adapts her to find what he calls home. The man who calls himself scientist will say it is sound, or the earth's magnetic field, or the way the sun hangs. He knows a pigeon created for air eventually comes down, divorced from origin. A man who calls himself scientist will say domestic pigeon when he means dove of peace; the man will say history between the domestic pigeon and man is ancient, will make it so her bones are hollow, body shaped to offer no resistance. He will make it so the pigeon is the way he calls adapted, so a nest is hers, is home. In this way, a pigeon is adapted to crouch so the man can mount. A pigeon returns, breeds with what is familiar. A man will make a pigeon adapted for two eggs, two glossy, two white; a man who calls himself scientist will make a pigeon adapted to lay only in the presence of the man, only when she can smell him. In this way a scientist who calls himself a man makes what he calls home. Over time she breeds year-round; years and years of two glossy, two white, into the nest that barely holds them. The pigeon waits in her nest of feces, mummified nestlings of the dead. This is what the man thinks the pigeon calls home. But a pigeon may sometimes lay eggs in the presence of hens. Sometimes she may lay eggs in the presence of no one at all. Over time she may lay her eggs but then she may sit on the roof, on the fence, on the other side of the balcony. A man might then say she is his dove, a white dove, light. When a man calls her dove, he will make it so her light becomes dark and her dark becomes light, her circadian rhythms change. This is progress. A man who calls himself scientist may lesion the pigeon, try to make it so she only remembers what he calls home but cannot find it. When released she will fly east, not north, not the way he calls away. She will ignore the pricks, an asterism part of a Great Bear, the way she could call home. He thinks she is blind without recent memory. But a man forgets the way it happened a long long time ago, how creation evolves beyond the man, his knowing.

THE MERE EXPOSURE EFFECT, OR HOW TO MAKE MEN LIKE YOU

Become an octopus, the kind that becomes
a flounder, at least enough like one to pass
as bottom feeder; flatten, for example
that tone of saying I'm fine when squeezed
between rock and bottom. You say when squeezed,
a flounder's eyes will shift to one side.
A fluke.

A floundering octopus can't watch her own back
when navigating minefields—lionfish
who ambush using elongated fins to corner
the thing that needs. Top predators who squeeze
also explode

invading territory that never once belonged to them.
It's well known lionfish pursue without warnings;
it's well known you will be well-liked
if you as an octopus are more like
the one who is doing the liking.
Mimicry is defence.

You will shape eight legs to look like spines,
become venom, say of others
just like you poor sole had it coming.
This is how octopus becomes lionfish,
invasive species invades
you, a bomb
will lose
its shell.

TO MY PEEPING TOM

I watched you watch me first,
sweaty pits,
thighs rubbing
together, in bed

always home before
the streetlamps
lit up. When you caught me

with your eyes did you
Photoshop my lips to coral,
hair to sun? Was I a devil
with a blue dress or a lady

in red? Did it matter
if I didn't like
pina coladas?

When I notice you now,
Buffalo Bill in the boardroom,
chatroom,
will you know I see you

seeing me everywhere
before I end up here on Fremont Street,
wondering if when you say false

fronts, you mean what's underneath
my shirt or just the architecture?
You say we have been here so long,
will we always be

together, instead of temporarily,
or is it all just
in how you look at it?
Vegas used to be the place to watch
the atomic bomb.

All those women,
pictured nightly,
dressed in tiny

mushroom clouds,
wondering if you know what
and who you're watching,
if it's going to be different this time,
if you've come
too close.

MISSED HER RIGHT

To pretty in pink
on the subway last night,
he thinks your mother told you never talk

to strangers; you must want
trimmed moustache wearing
mostly dark and handsome. Seemingly

aloof, were you burro taco waitress
pictured beautiful underneath
your uniform?

Remember him, the Prince
fan? You would know
him by his charming

purple socks;
and you the one
he wants to claim, like baggage

last red-eye flight in April.
You caught his same connection
staring at your front

page news, as if. Knew what he wanted
of you if you know what he means

drunk girl with pink hair in the Country Style.
He knows your mother
told you never talk in danger

even when you're not sure
if you're interested,
although he never asked

how many have there been
like him
you knew

should be anachronisms,
a time long long ago,
far far away
from you.

SOUND BITES

Lugosi in his coffin, typecast
by thickness of breath, threateningly
stiff, you played a rooster
in meat cinema; high power
shooter rifles, revolver cartridge
belts loaded, ready to unleash
the infection

of what exactly
you never figured out

surviving. When your father barked
you were just
his bitch, the son of
his howls for splatter
film worse than biting
the big one

on the way out.
From him learn cocks
and chicks in the farmhouse, your gun
in apocalyptic situations pointed
right between the lips, blow

out some brains;
that's how you come

to be a real man
up or else.

If you're gonna shoot
like a girl don't come crying

about things
that go bump in the night.
Whether the creature
featured in midnight madness marathons

or a man on the evening news,
give a command
performance,
never showing

fear. I'd watch you
wait for a round
of applause,

like handguns what you did with fists;
did you think it was just
SFX, the magic of movies,

you learning to crow
a choice between becoming

the zombie
or the gun.

THREE MONKEYS

I would bunker down saying I know
Bob and not
the masked man therefore
Bob is not
the masked man.
When selfless times called
for desperate pleasures
I thought I knew
myself
and you

in relation. The probability of two occurring
together is less than one
but still I tied
a knot with you, rings on fingers,
tin cans tied to bumper, an action
significant in itself or seemingly so,
the way monkeys look
in the mirror. After days of belting
aggressions they notice the inside
of his mouth, her tongue, what was two
creatures becoming
one, a mistaken

case of identity.
It was you
who taught me to know
suits, the kind
wolves hide in while I tell
myself the absence
of who I knew as Bob is not
you. Shearing sheep,
you tell me anything
with such thin skin deserves
the cold.

Comfort, my dear, is
now arms-length, a way
of measuring
our distance
at a highway
roadside diner robbery.

When your mask comes down
it's hands up,
or else maybe
a neutrino bomb.

These are fallacies I have used.
I say now I saw
not you,
heard nothing,
speak.

BEAUTY AND THE BEAST

My mother was Patty Hearst,
kidnapped by guerrillas.
Tell everyone I'm smiling

despite the dynamite.
They said she was in love,
posing with machine guns
for maximum publicity,
in front with fist-clenched salute.
She stood so no one saw

the real story, unnamed,
the mother of Jean de l'Ours, blindfolded
for a month at least
by bear with a boulder over
entrance to cave or closet—
it doesn't matter. In the middle
of a robbery in Stockholm

bear behaviour is predictable.
A bear, she said, will bluff,
will stoop to open mouth to show
oh what sharp teeth you have!

Don't show him yours.

If he slaps the ground,
circles with head high
it's going to be a real stick 'em up.

After, there are valentines,
roses. She has the petals
still. With gaping teeth in cheek,
she used to say in pictures now
you close your mouth; a bear bites
only to show
you are too close.

IMPOSSIBLE SPLIT, OR WHAT TO WEAR WHEN SURVIVING A LION ATTACK

I am wearing mother's red shoes
too small but for dancing,
directionless.

A gazelle will dance too,
will stot to show
how hard she is
how fast.

I am wearing mother's red nails
painted fragile, cupped upward
in open prayer, ears are still listening
instead of a fist, unable to grip.

A gazelle will pronk too,
like dancing is joyous,
like dancing is not
endorphins that numb.

I am wearing mother's red lips, split
to the pit like a cherry
with stem I'm supposed to tie
in knots while speaking.
The stem stays silent.

In forty-five seconds a lion sinks
his teeth into a neck,
less than the time
between two heartbeats

I am wearing mother's red voice
the one that is quietly full
of blood, but always quiet.

A lion does not know how
gazelles play dead.
She shivers,
gets up, forgets.
She does not know how.

Red shoes will take me this way or any way other
than how I want to go, no stopping; no choice
but to dance frenetic

or cut them off.

PENDULUM

At first feel your body getting sleepy, getting heavy. Follow the way a finger points, backwards to younger you a man said was his dream, all high-heeled breasts or hot cutoff lips, a siren but no wailing. He wants to take this. He'll say it's basic, how could he resist, after asking a pocket watch to show your yes, the pendulum moving circular straight lines, near, away. When you wake you won't remember; ask a pocket watch to show him your no, and he says *try to see it through my eyes*. It will swing in a straight line, in maybe a different direction but still a lot like yes. He says hypnosis is science; anyone can resist.

Next feel your body getting heavy, feel your body get older, and emotion is for the thing called relationship. And how could you resist bright Sunday morning over eggs, your hands being held, together, on Saturdays, dancing cheek to cheek. How could you resist turning the other cheek, promise of white fence, even when topped with chicken wire for always and ever now that you're just that little bit older, still, the promise of your eggs on Sunday mornings in bed. You are losing all sense of time. And do you take this as woman? When you wake you won't remember any of this; Kool-Aid and other promises sliding, like butter sticks down the back of your throat. Hypnosis relaxes the gag reflex.

Then feel your body in dead stop, sinking through the floor. Now that you're older, your yes or no may be clockwise or counterclockwise circles instead of straight lines. When swinging a bat you were taught to lead with the hips. When it comes to the pendulum your yes might also be deadstopped. You might walk down an aisle, all left together, stop, right together, stop; hypnosis is caused by a loss of equilibrium. *And do you take this woman?* He might want you to squawk like a chicken, sing like Elvis, then you'll stay put, stay still. He might want you to stay unbalanced; you know hitting in baseball is the same as a knockback, the recoil from a gun. In any case, you are to remain stationary.

Now try to feel your body. You won't remember how he made you go hot; he can make you go cold. You won't remember becoming a human plank, rigid so a man can sit on your stomach, how you became a placeholder for your name. Settling is the process of staying in place the way a fence rots so it no longer leads to the road. On average you'll sleep for twenty-five years; you won't remember why you ever counted sheep. If you wake you might remember the ones that have jumped, the ones that used to lead to dreams.

EVEN THIS POEM IS BLUE

Like everyone else think I'm still attached
to being a lovely hand attached to a lovely
wrist attached to a lovely hole
in the ground

I keep digging myself. And it's not getting any
younger you know, the hole, I mean; it doesn't eat
whole foods or clean dirt from its pores, doesn't
get enough sleep, especially on its bright side.
But how would a hole know which way is up?
Lots of men do

assume what a hole needs. It's a hole so eventually
it will need to be filled, the question is with what
or who and how much of it will be with the ones
that are not in the hole; they always ask about the hole.
They always ask are you even trying to get out of this hole?
Are we even trying? Then sometimes they try
with aces or pies or pegs, square or otherwise.

This they call nesting, which is also a hole
as if I was a ferret or badger or bee
whose knees are suddenly weakened
by the gravity of understanding
that the sky I used to see outside the hole was not really
blue, but refracted that way; the sky a part of a bigger sky
with too many holes made by you and me and others like me
who liked me really but outside of that there was nothing

except space,
the part between
hole and absorption
into density,
the payoff of being unfilled
so many times the weight
of one misspelled
sun.

THE STARTER

If a spiny lobster has no claws
does it mean she'll know her place?
A lobster condo under a scrap car hood
or junked fridge. She craves shelter,
casita you presume she dreams of,
if lobsters dream. You say
there's no evidence it's not
about dinner, being together
in small spaces, compressed gas.
I'm telling you it takes two divers
to free a lobster like this. There is
the risk of nitrogen narcosis,
other reversible alterations
of consciousness. No evidence
it's love. When diving there is the risk
of flipping the top of a little house
we can't keep from falling apart
or backwards like the sky, another
story you say doesn't matter now;
we're already submerged.

NIGHTS OF THE LIVING POSSUM

Playing dead was easier
than out running
a creature of Romero
so she stayed

on that infamous balcony
scene. With sayings from survivors
of suburbia she got
into the act

of our own genealogical
experiment gone
wrong

when two didn't quite make
a right. Left

alone with baby she barricaded
windows, made realistic
panic in one-nine-hundred phone calls
psychically trying to predict

the next outbreak. The marsupial
on our porch birthed offspring
crawling blind
across the mother's belly, infiltrating

her again. When there are too many,
some don't make it.

My mother knew surviving
by succumbing

to the bite,
bit by bit,
a zombie walk

made for a
child can kill
its mother.
Dead

or terrified, this pouched
mammal sick
from carrying,
but they never asked
what have you outlived only
what have you become?

THE TRUE CONFESSIONS OF BUFFALO BILL

On t.v. in the basement watch dad
as Buffalo Bill's night vision—
girls and holes, butterflies
in throats, woman
suited

for the keeping. Like Bill
he used to skin his humps;
my mother's arms
in baby blue like movies meant I never wanted
to walk inside her skin
or shoes. Like Brudo's from the junkyard, worn
out when no one
could see, he left
his mark

where shoes pinched space
between her foot
and my killer's heel.

Don't be
a pussy stuck
in a hole.

Thick skin
is a dead thing,
the way a camel

cannibalizes its humps. I refused
to see protuberant guns,
knives or chainsaws spreading
girls open

but honestly, she asked *would you fuck me?*
Yeah I'd fuck

sideways, horizontally,
lay our bodies
at the morgue
for listening

to how Buffalo Bill
was just
an urban legend.

SPECIMEN

I was told all toads are thin skinned;
moist is perfect for the letting in directly
to the bloodstream, a defining

characteristic of the boys I knew when we played
doctor. Show me yours and I'll show you
how a frog looks

spread out, pinned down.
I learned boys cut what they can't
lick. Afterwards, I felt clammy
like in the princess story of losing
a ball down a well,
tongues on an object

that even when blown out, aroused the fear
of catching flies like mother said would happen
with legs splayed like that. Later

clams and frogs are delicacies of experimentation
for consumption. I am considered
only like dead things
but I have not forgotten
how to also cut a daddy

long legs so he can't
grow
back.

ON MY MOTHER'S TERMS

Body was porcelain, the shell
named after a pig's vagina.
Marble is harder, but still,
a man-made Venus, busted
in transport, chest
intact. Consider
the structure;

body is used
here as object
the same as becoming
the carrying part

of passenger craft, a ship
like Orellana's
searching for cinnamon

instead finds Amazon, a word
for woman, antagonistic or equal
or full-breasted or one,
the kind of either or
that makes a term mean
both and nothing

mother warned about. The Amazons
cauterized defining parts
in order to shoot an arrow. I know this split.
I have never felt
inside my body, always miss

represented, watched
through glass eyes,
a mass of matter distinct
from others, but defined still
in relation, my terror

of prepositions, conjunctions.
Mother said women like Amazons
and her and me
were supposed to be women
with children. Still

at least you'll be loved;
Tit for tat.
Language is a funny thing
when it comes to breasts;
no way a woman
should have or could have
survived

my mother said,
what the Amazons described.

WHEN READING HAMLET IN MY THIRTIES I ANSWERED FOR GERTRUDE

Some of us used
pineapples, left hanging

pictures of a pomegranate
or got rubbed down

with garlic to see if our mouths
would smell the same.

Sometimes we inserted dates,
our fruit quite literally

way up there,
or else it was red nitre, the kind

of ash Egyptians used
for drying out their mummies.

Sometimes it was done to us,
those Romans spanking brides,

an Argo going Marvin Gay
on virgins in the mountains,

same way that U.S. seamen came
to fight a war, without protection. Mostly

they were using us
to make themselves but smaller, mostly

it was dangerous,
a motive to start drinking

whether beer and baboon urine
or a toxic Spanish Fly

made to swell down there.
In every case it led to hemorrhage,

all tears and blood and milk,
no honey. Let's not pretend

it's not a question of to be
or to beget. I'm told don't try to fight the urge

like magnetism,
a clock that's ticking

two minutes to midnight they say
my body lives downwind

of mushroom clouds
should feel

even in comparison, a poem
is really small.

OF WEATHERING VIEWED THROUGH THE EYELETS OF A SPOON BUSK

These functional impairments by erosion of rocks are viewed
as flower pots when viewed
from the water, viewed recurrently when waves
crash. He defines the interpersonal
problems in relations summarized
by a goldfish swimming
on her back

or backed in a corner,
the attic, a room not her own. A stay
that tightens like whale bone
or Adam impair
the function of ribs,
diminishing
effects

of a small smooth glove
that used to hold
a hand, understanding
before a
border

line defining
pervasive patterns
of deficits, numbing
all fire he says
she is just a wet blanket
statement recurrent;
the trick is conviction.
He'll say it like
he means it.
So when he means,

it diminishes the effects
of feeling.
She knows she was plenty

of fish in
a bucket, now she wants
to kick
it she wants
don't
shoot

THE ACCIDENT

When I didn't kill the baby

raccoon who crossed the road
my mother said I was a natural

mistake. No instinct, didn't know
survival. You are a woman now

so don't
wear overalls, stay away
from grocery stores and parking lots
between the hours of five and eight.

If eggs are thrown
at your window do not start
the wipers or spray
water. The milk
will block your view

of the killer who could be
in the back seat.

Security comes at the cost of worry—
long hair and ponytails,
maybe bun or gift
from the Klingerman Foundation.

When you have your own children
you'll understand, maintain a healthy
fear of anthrax, suspect
all bundles delivered
by air mail. They'll come

unexpected as roadkill.
She never saw it

coming,
her bundle of joy;

tread marks revealing
her direction, steering

off anywhere
somewhere other

than here,
than mother, before

the accident.

MIRROR MIRROR
MOTHER MOTHER

Mother's angles
are light scattered
convexly so she's never
tall. Look the right way
you see a mother that was
in heels with vacuum, a hug
that never creased,
long-shattered except
mother still feels

a string of pearls she
has to be fairer than.

Everything reflects in accordance
to when he comes home
and who mother is
is only a part

of the visible spectrum.
In black and white
She is both
mother

            and the other
            who wished
            on the magic apple
            one bite and what
            if I had not

            if my children were not
            may all your
            dreams come
            instead

mother will sleep little,
read less, dream

chalk fingers
marking the wall,

the sentence of mother
will mother. After all,
other mothers do.

    What others do unseen, but heard
    in resonant frequency
    shatters the mirror
    a mother
    in two.

AS TOLD DURING A ROUTINE POLICE INVESTIGATION

My mother was a secret Shahrazad,
a trick of the tongue.

The holes
in the wall he made at home became
ways to worlds underground,
the tale of a djinn trapped in a bottle too small
to hold a big toe; I listened

while bruises on her arm went
black as fish,
guts out
on the counter,
his knuckle inside.

She said they became jewelled
when the djinn
was tricked back
in the lamp, so I waited

while my mother stayed
home in the dark of the day.

Girls turned to dogs, then bitches, whipped,
when forty or thirty-three thieves stole
one thousand days and nights.
All part of the story, I

waited
for red letters,
yelled to let her
open sesame.

Even now I do not know
the watchword
for staying out
of a jar.

DELUSIONAL DOMINATING PERSONALITY DISORDER

If a real man's a cowboy
he can't be a syndrome.

Father's John Wayne wears a hat
into a syllogism. At high noon
a real man casts a shadow—
but only a mouse draws a gun
at night. He cast a shadow,

watched it cover walls, thumbs pointed inward
to the envy of my father, guns drawn
at the ready and waiting to shoot down
thin skins or paper tigers.

The weak
Wayne knew
needed no
apologizing.

If you cast a shadow
you can draw a gun at night.

You'll get yourself killed talking that way,
pilgrim. You're in for a troubled youth. Lost
boys making women out of pixelated pornos,
think their strength is in penumbra, in never
feeling the way a clay pigeon shatters, a duck
sits down, rolls over, exposing what used to be

only a mouse

who draws a gun at night

a real man

SISTER/HOOD

So many times,
we've watched
Kitty in a corner
forced to last tango
sob story
so many
watching
no one
made the call.

THE POLITICS OF LEFTOVERS

Nonna's dialect is missing
the word for no. Cut
such a thin slice
of whatever it's barely

a piece to eat. You're too thin.
With hair shaved down like that
you look like no nice boy
will ever want

a piece. Assume no
to eating sausage,
homemade by passing through the hands
of women in my family
forbidden from eating out

at Burger King. In the bathrooms,
a girl my age is missing
on a poster beside
someone's pet cat.
Think about everyone else
who's thought about

licking the coconut
sunscreen off her back.
I was always still hungry,

for what exactly, young lady
do you mean
by acting like
you're excused?

Just have it, a trifle,
the lives of girls and women
having grandkids,
a little spongy in the middle
like nonna made for Christmas.

ON THE PROCESS OF MAKING OMELETTES

Picture conversation,
old t.v. set in black and white
antenna or breakfast, scrambled

the difference between bombshells
and eggshells. Red-blooded males
don't eat lettuce. It's sterile.

So learn to live
with fear,
consuming

relationships
are a lot like food.

First slow heat, then
it comes down to ova
always getting broken

up. Every time an egg cracked,
he justifies her yolk
forgotten, soft,

underneath.

GESTATIONAL STAGE

Did you believe me like you believe the Discovery
Channel when I said a woman like a seal comes
to ground only
to breed and nurse

like Doris Lessing
with her baby boy, trapped
but behaving beautifully

despite the sharks?
Letting go is hard to do.
Especially when there are teeth.

When we met you knew
your place on the food chain,
that sealskin key chain was better
than a rabbit's foot
you said; let's get lucky. You knew

the patterns of the hunt,
how a man knows to wait
for her white coat to become
ragged, how a seal becomes
just womb and breast, a pup feeding from
fat stores underneath her skin. You knew

for months and years
a seal will not see
the mouths that eat her,
take her outsides leaving
her locked in her skin locked in
a trunk, a longing
to remember
how to swim.

I said they used to use
seal blubber for light,
fetal tissue to power
electric generators; when we talked
about it we talked around
it. It was never
him or her.

Just teeth, a tiny tail
paddling against
the current because

you could not believe
when I said sometimes
a seal departs from her usual
diet of cephalophods, birds, small fish.

Sometimes she'll
eat a shark slowly,
from the inside.

THE EMERGENCY MANOEUVRES OF BLUEBEARD 6

Once upon a time there was and was not a little black box not
nothing but nothing you could see. A princess is a girl taught
not look in the little black box. If she can't see it, it won't exist.
Same way a dog descended from wolf who is shocked won't notice
the unelectrified side of the fence. This is the story I heard
from a friend of a friend of a friend who saw it with her own eyes:

A man who was and was not a prince taught a girl not to see a rat.
A man who was and was not a prince taught a girl not to see a black box.

I heard from a friend of a friend that in eight hundred years a story
doesn't change
until a planes goes down, leaves only the black box which is not black at all
but orange, bright, but easy to miss like the unelectrified side of the fence.
I didn't see it. But it exists.

DOPPELGANGER

It took me a long time to live
with my cunt like
Frankenstein's monster, the one
no one remembers
by name.

I was nine on the subway when the first guy grabbed
me. He blamed pesticides,
polychlorinated biphenyls and bisphenol A,
don't you look pretty because of precocious
gonadotrophin-releasing hormone chest sacs,
so much more important than facial recognition.

Such pretty little parts.
I had to watch

my twin stranger in heautoscopy, body
at a distance, but flat without
heat.

He said everyone interacts
like this
with girls
as they appear.

Naked in front of the mirror I saw mountains
where there should have been molehills.
In gym there were gonads,
the women's hidden up inside;
like everything else I never let a man see

I got good at not recognizing
the signs of Capgras
delusion. It's so natural, he said,
even back in ancient Egypt they knew there could be two,

the girl the same as me with memories identical
but impostor; the one who'll always say to men

but I love you

when I bleed.

YO YO FOR BEGINNERS

We keep getting on
and off and on with it,
like a bike, that time

on the octopus ride,
a study in centrifugal force.
Nails pressed to elbows,

pressing us to the cage.
We were always going to fall.
You said it only looks that way.

Apparent force,
always equal
and opposite

the way I turned,
you turned away.

You never quite got chemistry
in Kraft Dinner
together

with tiny hot dogs, falling in
bed beside,
and not around.

Lacking GPS, I calculate
our radius, take impact
statements, watch the rest

leach below
the water table.
Sinking under

saturated ground
you've become
too much to hold.

We'd always said no
kids. As if it was a joke. As if

when you cut tentacles
an octopus won't continue,
moving in the same exact direction
go so far to feed
a mouth that isn't.

DIFFERENTIAL DIAGNOSIS

In the past two weeks how often
have you called a wolf a bush,
black dogs just blues

beaten around the mountain
of dishes?
There are no molehills

in flattened dumps,
not being able
to climb out of bed, still

how often do you
paint your face in shades of pina colada,
mimic curvature

of upside down umbrellas,
pretend there are no clouds
like mushrooms

not that anyone else
can see. Make it
beautiful;

every day is supposed to be
a thousand white paper birds,
folded upwards,

now creased until cracked,
faces wet
with rain.

ON NOT HAVING A BABY

Crayons aren't eco-friendly;
there's no colony on Mars.

The end, according to the Mayans,
was supposed to start on Sunday.

Still we're due in 2026. At night,
I lie awake expecting

bomb threats in Hawaii, rising
levels of alerts, or of estrogen

in fish. False alarm. Be rational,
you say. If it happens, it happens.

There is no Punnett square to determine
whether my alleles, if wrong

can ever make a right,
the chances of expressing

phenotypic probability,
mother's tendencies to cut

her fingers, pick up every piece
of glass along the sidewalk,

still terrified somehow
of a sliver in a bottle,

the damage to stray dogs.
If you keep on breaking

strong glass, eventually
you get sand.

The smallest fraction,
broken further, in theory the distance

between her and me gets infinitely
small, while never being reached.

No one tries this with Russian roulette.
Be rational. Why take the chance

dividing two by two, my daughter
will not get my teeth

my bark, my bite,
just the loss

of expecting
sleep.

CHOOSE YOUR OWN ADVENTURE

Mother's alter ego, alias
grace lurking underneath
the kitchen counter and me
sitting in tutu talking suffragettes,
swatting flies off little pink houses
fighting the power of Grayskull
with a woman's right to choose
pie or crumble buildings
with a single bound.
As if

when Wonder Woman ran for president
we could all parry bullets with our bracelets,
while the taking care of was taken care of.
As if

being a wonder full woman was not a story
about a princess' marriage at bedtime;
my mother wanting another ending.
Wonder Woman never breast fed; She-Ra
never made it back for dinner, never mind
in time to start what should be started.
As if

a girl could fly in amber, hardened tree sap
over time. Things will always be,
my mother said, preserved, greyer
against static, the background;
even a fly can see the illusion
of motion when there is none,
that tiny movement.
Secret.

IF THE LEFT KNEE ITCHES

A toad was bad luck, a man
who will make other men believe
when a bone from a toad is put
into a woman's dress it will kindle,
turning her tiger. He'll say, c'mon
you'd fuck her. You don't believe
a tiger's whiskers are poison
or that black cat crap; just grab
the pussy cat, that lady
is a tramp. You can kiss anything
with tic tacs. If a woman's knee itches
it means she's fond of men
or bad luck. Never mind knees
together, a pretty picture
dropping to them, I knew
you'd flip your top for me. He'll say
he never said it doesn't matter
what a woman says, as long as it's young
and beautiful, using I-messages
to describe a break in the femur,
bad luck. He forgets a dog digging
in dirt means a storm. He forgets
if a toad bites a man to make it let go
it makes it rain boiling water,
makes it pour.

BY OMISSION

What he's saying is not
about exposure,
a negative

conveyed
on a strip, super
imposed on another image

of what happened to some Monroe
in black panties for black ties;
she got pinned

like butterflies
on film
that change the light whether white

is black or black is white
he'll argue
he's due

process;
there are always shades
of grey that remain the same.

Regardless if the image is positive
or negative, delicately
handled by

sincerely
appreciating how extremely
sorry he remains in the dark

room. All locker talk
he'll argue
his image

was never
inappropriately
exposed without a con-

sensual attachment. Flashbulb
is a kind of memory he knows
his hands,

saturated
in groping,
a blur of what was hers, so still

not his to touch. When viewed
through a certain lens he forgets
her face,

mannequin
made by autofocus,
compression used

to reduce is never lossless. In theory
he's saying two negatives give a positive
except

when exposed by a blowout,
acting to cut the power

so the current
problem

is fixed so he can't not see.
Just look

at our resolution.

WITCH HUNT

Way back when all the nuns began
to bite or meow like cats together
authorities said it was natural

during the plagues that came
before the women danced
for days without rest, starving, riddled

hot blood a disease in all cases cured
if the woman was kept in processional,
like any other mass hysteria. Most died

in Salem; it happens sometimes because
of some fungi but not a witch
authorities think little girls rarely say

what they mean, when she said he said
and she said he did as the Halifax slasher
they said no proof of either a man

or his razor, well maybe there was
just not in that way we would test for it
not just believe what was said

was different from silence but still
we don't know to believe little girls
are allowed to mean.

GENERALIZED DISORDER

The problem with me you
said is irrational—

a number like pi
eyed from a distance, a fractal repeating
forever, seemingly random
yet self-
adjusting. Normal
has yet to be
proven but you expect
nothing less

than never being
out on a ledge or limb.
The problem

with me you said
is settling

for my permanent repeating
pattern of difficulty.
Like snakeskin you said,
too taut, unable
to follow the flow, shedding

only crocodile tears.
What you mean is the problem
is reptilian, a lizard lodged
in my dendrites,
a series of actions
equal and opposite to
all of what could have should have
been.

Try to reduce
worry to a fraction lacking

a common denominator,
the addition of us becoming

impossible. With me you do not see
the problem
with you

you do not see the ground
adjusting between us
the problem

by definition reduces
to absurd.

ON EXITING THE LOOP

To understand recursion, you must understand
recursion; the pattern continues at even
the smallest scale, the image of a woman
holding cocoa holds an object
containing her smaller
image. The effect
of appearing to herself
in a place where a similar
her would realistically be
expected to appear, means
in each iteration
she is reduced

to a fraction of what she was before.
Apply, for example, fractal analysis to the tango;
when you led you stepped on her
so she had to step back. Words were had, repeating
like how if you look
closely at the pattern inherent
in words like crazy or bitch
you find bit, you find cry.
To the viewer this continues
only as long
as the resolution

allows. To the viewer a maze
or relationship means proceeding
until a woman reaches either an exit,
or branching point; she must try each one.
If they all lead to dead
ends put things
in perspective.
At least they say
she had a man to want

to make up with. But this is not
from the perspective of a woman boxed

with cocoa powder; a doll
from the perspective
of the viewer stacked inside
another doll inside
what is a dark place

from the perspective of the doll
appears different. You'll say
it's all in how you look
at things,

but having been a little wooden doll, a matchstick
girl burning with no kindling
to find warmth

with you; she knows the definition
of doing the same thing over again expecting

differently you'd understand
recursion, eventually

you must

BRIARS

There are lots of things that prick:
stilettos the colour of sex lips
or cactus, how a girl met
a boy, or a girl met a needle;
once upon a time

there's a twirling spindle
or dart gun injecting elephants
with LSD. A splinter underneath nail
can make a PET scan bright red
with need

like a prick makes a heroine's normal
a catheter pumping
at unpredictable intervals
barbituates directly
into the stomach.

For little match girls
when there's nothing left
to burn, the way
to see a shadow
is find where edges fade,
where there used to be
more than no more
but now not.

ME TOO

If you could create one sound,
just one to register
at over one
thousand decibels
you would create
a black hole with potential
to take out our entire planet
plus ones potentially
surrounding us.

You bet they'd hear that one in the woods.

LAWS OF MOTION

Bodies in motion remain emotion
less as bodies in relationship. The relationship
will be described between a body here
and your body hereinafter referred to
as the object when acted upon by force.
This has yet to be proven but the maximum
amount of force a body can exert
on another object given the gravity
of the situation is a constant, as is the length
of a skirt. Can you tell us for example
how you were blind drunk or not to the angle
at which your body would be viewed as a thing
of a liar especially dressed like that?
We calculate the distance between knees inversely
proportional to a proximal cause
of resistance you ought to have known
about attraction equal and opposite
under the law when a body chooses
to enter the room of another body
it's only force if there's resistance
beyond a reasonable doubt you ought
to have known how force can result
from contact or non-contact. But tell us
how if it was force why were there cuddles
and talking why here and after, the contact?
These are deemed inadmissible changes in emotion used
against the tendency of a body that remains
at rest. Tell us how your object here
and after referred to as the objection
your honour, that was never made
because of how after it was over your body
remained at rest we can prove when it comes
to inertia you cannot fire a bullet in a vacuum;
if friction can be eliminated so can the resistance.
This is where the case will rest until it is shown
resistance can be an invisible force until

we doubt false laws until
we listen to you,
the proof.

EXTINCTION

Consider how to most safely go. Consider a bird in a cage or consider a woman. Consider the bird is trained by a man to peck at the ball that looks like an egg, consider she is trained to push it. At first the man will reward every time, then some of the time, then very little of the time at all. Consider a woman trained by a man to be in love. She may push and she may push and then he may push and push and push back. In this way, a bird learns to get food, a woman learns to receive a thing called love, a pigeon learns to play ping pong.

Identify safe friends and safe places. Consider the pigeon is fed for being near the ball she thought was an egg; the pigeon is fed for pushing the ball to the other side of the table. Next the pigeon is not fed, next the pigeon is shocked. The pigeon is shocked by a man, the one who used to feed her. Extinction is how the behaviour disappears. The man who is a scientist will say the dinosauriformes underwent extinction. A ball of fire catapulted towards them, caterpillars starved herbivores by eating all plants, or else they were subsumed in ice. Practice an escape route.

Know where you'll go, even if you don't think you'll have to. The homing pigeon evolved to find her way home; Darwin said she could be bred. Darwin said, so during wartime Cher Ami delivered men's messages; during wartime she lost a leg, had bullets lodged in her chest. During wartime, he forgot she was she, the one who was trained to be dear; the man who taught pigeons to play ping pong made them guide torpedoes.

Stay close to the exits. He identifies the first extinction as accident, but the woman remembers how volcanoes erupted, released selenium. The woman remembers volcanoes which thinned the eggs, millions and millions of unborn eggs, what seemed like the promise of future, gone when the shells were so thin they cracked. The scientist will identify the accident as extinction, he will not see how the eggs were changed. It takes seven trials for the pigeon to stop pecking completely, for the observable behaviour to stop being observed. Build on what you're doing to survive.

Trust your instincts. The pigeon evolved from another pigeon, one who did not know torpedoes; the pigeon evolved to find her way home. The dinosauriformes changed into birds. Years later, thousands, they learned to fly.

ACKNOWLEDGEMENTS

"D.C. AL CODA (FROM THE HEAD TO THE TAIL)" and "RATIONING" first appeared in *The Fiddlehead, Issue 276, Summer Poetry, Summer 2018.*

"FIRST GIRL/FINAL GIRL" first appeared in *Third Point Press, Issue 8 (Skin).*

"GESTATIONAL STAGE" first appeared in *Carte Blanche, Issue 33, Summer 2018.*

"GOING SOUTH" first appeared in *Bad Dog Review, Issue 1.*

"LAWS OF MOTION" first appeared in *The Puritan, Issue 40, Winter 2018.*

"LET'S TALK" first appeared in *CV2, 41.4, Spring 2019.*

"ON NOT HAVING A BABY" first appeared in *The Puritan, Issue 44, Winter 2019.*

"PRIME TIME HORROR STORY" first appeared in *New Poetry.*

"THINGS SHE WANTS" first appeared in *Minola Review, Issue 15.*

"WEDDING DAY, CIRCA MY MOTHER" first appeared in *The Temz Review, Issue 1.*

"FIRST GIRL / FINAL GIRL," "THINGS SHE WANTS," "THE ACCIDENT," "TO MY PEEPING TOM," "THE TRUE CONFESSIONS OF BUFFALO BILL," "AS TOLD DURING A ROUTINE POLICE INVESTIGATION," "DOPPELGANGER," "GENERALIZED DISORDER," AND "EXTINCTION" appeared together in the chapbook *The True Confessions of Buffalo Bill (Anstruther Press,* 2018.)

Thank you to *Mansfield Press* and to Denis De Klerck, for all your insights that made this a better book.

Thank you to Robin Richardson for your mentorship, your invaluable editing, your encouragement, and your belief in these poems all the way at the beginning.

Thank you to Jim Johnstone for suggestions that made many of these pieces so much stronger. Thank you to Kathryn Mockler for being such an encouraging teacher.

Thank you to everyone in the Unsympathetic Poetry Workshops, and the Eastwood Writer's Collective for your feedback, your support, and your sense of community.

Thank you to my partner Mat. Without you, this would not have been possible.

Thank you, as always, to my mother.

Photo: Pat Bolduc

Paola Ferrante is a writer and teacher who has a chapbook with *Anstruther Press* and has published poetry and fiction in *The Puritan, CV2, The Fiddlehead, Room, Joyland*, and elsewhere. She won *Room*'s prize for fiction, and was shortlisted for *PRISM International*'s Grouse Grind. She is currently the Poetry Editor at *Minola Review* and resides in Toronto, Canada, with her partner Mat, and her two pet ferrets.